To Sam Parkes   M.L.

To Sarah-Jane, Joanna, and Matthew   K.L.

Published by
The Dial Press
1 Dag Hammarskjold Plaza
New York, New York 10017

First published in Great Britain
by Methuen/Walker Books

Library of Congress Cataloging in Publication Data
Lane, Margaret, 1907–   The fox.
Summary: Introduces the physical characteristics, habits, and behavior
of foxes and explains how they hunt for food and raise their young.
1. Red fox—Juvenile Literature. [1. Foxes]
I. Lilly, Kenneth, ill. II. Title. III. Series
QL737.C22L26 1982   599.74′442   82-71355
ISBN 0-8037-2491-8   AACR2

THE FOX

By Margaret Lane

Pictures by
Kenneth Lilly

THE DIAL PRESS/New York

Foxes live by their wits. If they were not cunning and skilled, they would have disappeared long ago, like many other animals who were trapped and hunted. But today red or common foxes are thriving in the United States and Canada, in Europe and North Africa. People are their only enemy, but foxes have worked out many successful ways to live close to them without being discovered.

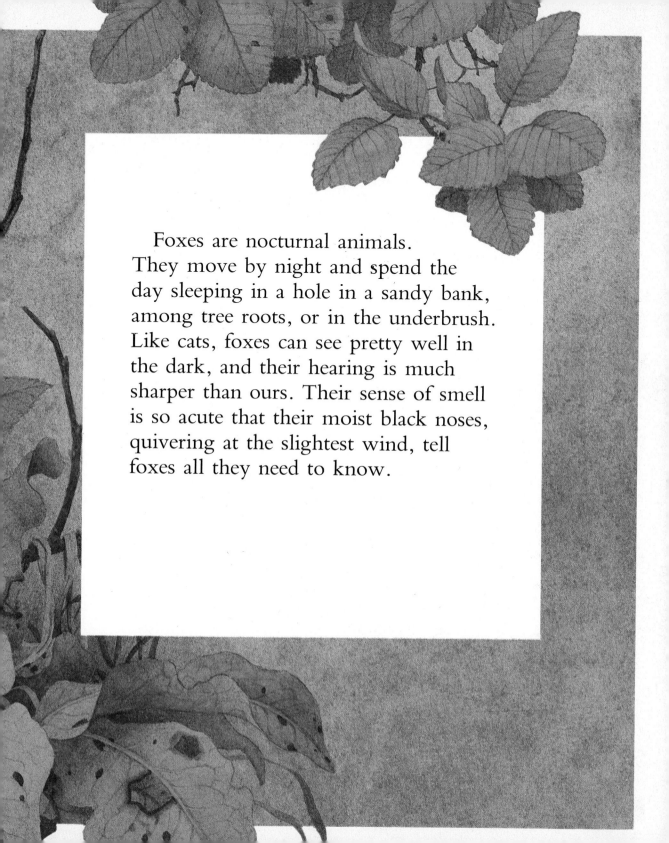

Foxes are nocturnal animals.
They move by night and spend the
day sleeping in a hole in a sandy bank,
among tree roots, or in the underbrush.
Like cats, foxes can see pretty well in
the dark, and their hearing is much
sharper than ours. Their sense of smell
is so acute that their moist black noses,
quivering at the slightest wind, tell
foxes all they need to know.

Foxes do not live permanently in families. The male or dog fox is a solitary animal, ranging and hunting in an area he has staked out as his own. It is the female fox, the vixen, who feeds and looks after her cubs until they are old enough to hunt and survive by themselves. She, unlike the dog fox, may keep to a particular hole for long periods, perhaps even two or three years. She does not like hard digging, so she usually takes over a hole dug by rabbits or badgers and enlarges it to suit her own needs.

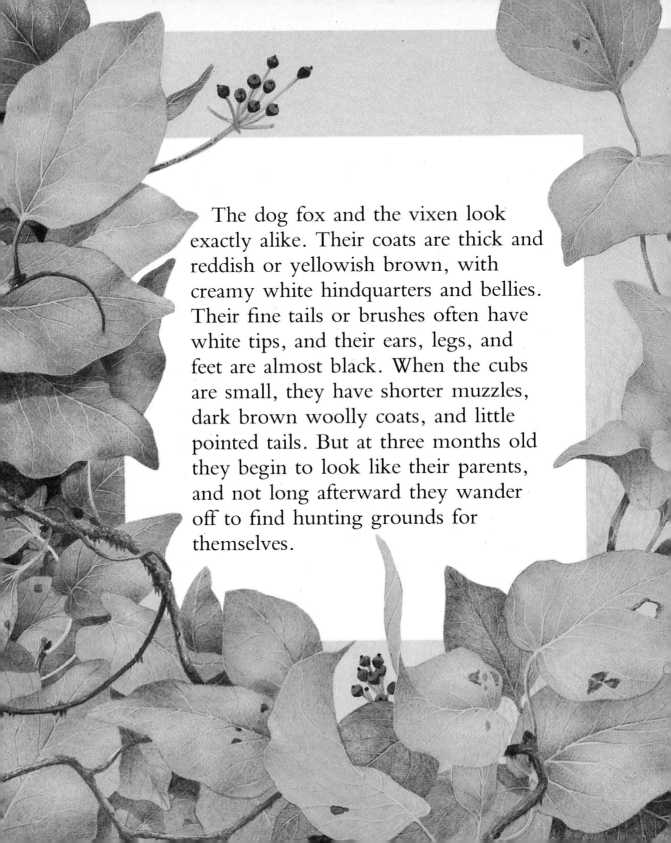

The dog fox and the vixen look exactly alike. Their coats are thick and reddish or yellowish brown, with creamy white hindquarters and bellies. Their fine tails or brushes often have white tips, and their ears, legs, and feet are almost black. When the cubs are small, they have shorter muzzles, dark brown woolly coats, and little pointed tails. But at three months old they begin to look like their parents, and not long afterward they wander off to find hunting grounds for themselves.

The foxes' breeding time is in winter, when the vixen makes her weird calls— more like the scream of a peacock than a dog's bark. This is a signal to all dog foxes nearby. They run quickly to her and fight one another, rearing up on their hind legs and gnashing their teeth fiercely. The vixen may mate with more than one, but the courting season is brief. When she ceases to call, the dog foxes depart. The dominant male may stay in the area for a while, without sharing his mate's hole or taking much interest in her.

About two months later three, four, or perhaps five cubs will be born. They are blind at first and look more like kittens than foxes. Their mother nurses them for at least four weeks, leaving the hole only to find food for herself. When they are about a month old, the cubs begin to come out, romping and playing near the entrance while the vixen watches. They stalk and pounce on one another, practicing the skills they will need in the wild. The vixen brings them mice, beetles, and worms to eat, and when they are three months old, the cubs try catching their own food.

Foxes lead solitary lives because food is hard to come by and each one needs a separate hunting ground. Rabbits are a favorite meal, but they are difficult to catch. Rats, voles, mice, and frogs are easier prey, as are birds that nest on the ground. Foxes eat eggs when they can find them and dig beetles out of cow dung. They also like ripe berries, and in farming country a stray duck or hen is a special treat. This makes farmers foxes' enemies, but hunters are even more dangerous to them. Even though people kill and eat poultry and wild birds, they become furious when foxes do the same.

Luckily for foxes, their sense of smell is so sharp that they can catch the scent of a person a long way off. They always know who or what is in their area. However foxes leave their own scent as well, and this works against them. To stake out their territory foxes urinate on bushes and posts, and they have scent glands in the pads of their feet. These scents enable hunters' hounds to follow a fox through fields and woods. Without them they would never find the fox's hidden paths and lairs.

Fox hunting is not as old a sport as many people believe. In earlier times there were not enough foxes to be worth chasing, and rabbits and deer were the common prey of hunters. But gradually the number of foxes increased, and fox hunting became popular. It is not a very easy sport, because foxes have many cunning methods of escape. They will mingle with a flock of sheep, run along roads, or swim across ponds and streams to conceal their scent.

The farmer has always been the fox's enemy. People think that as well as stealing poultry, foxes will also kill young lambs. But many more lambs are probably killed by dogs, who love chasing sheep and often run in packs. If foxes find dead or dying lambs, they will of course eat them, and there is no doubt they will kill a stray when they can find one. But hunters want foxes left for their own sport, and they bring pressure on farmers not to destroy them.

So foxes have gradually become more numerous, although thousands are still hunted and killed each year. Foxes continue to use their wits. As the human population increases and towns get bigger, they have discovered that they can live well in the suburbs. There neither farmers nor hunters threaten them and they can snatch food from garbage cans and bird feeders in backyards.

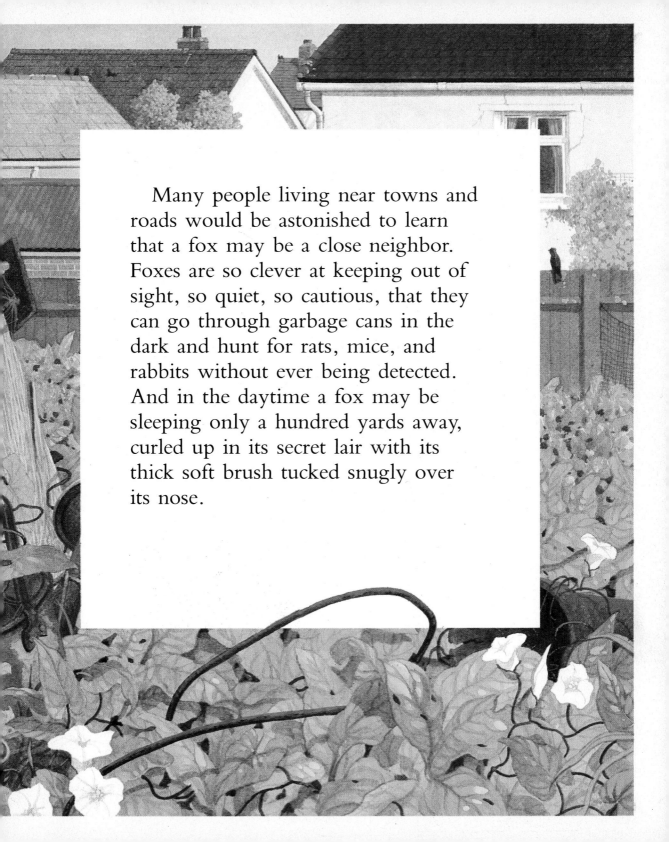

Many people living near towns and roads would be astonished to learn that a fox may be a close neighbor. Foxes are so clever at keeping out of sight, so quiet, so cautious, that they can go through garbage cans in the dark and hunt for rats, mice, and rabbits without ever being detected. And in the daytime a fox may be sleeping only a hundred yards away, curled up in its secret lair with its thick soft brush tucked snugly over its nose.